Persian, Greek And Roman Rule

Ancient Egypt History 4th Grade
Children's Ancient History

Speedy Publishing LLC
40 E. Main St. #1156
Newark, DE 19711
www.speedypublishing.com

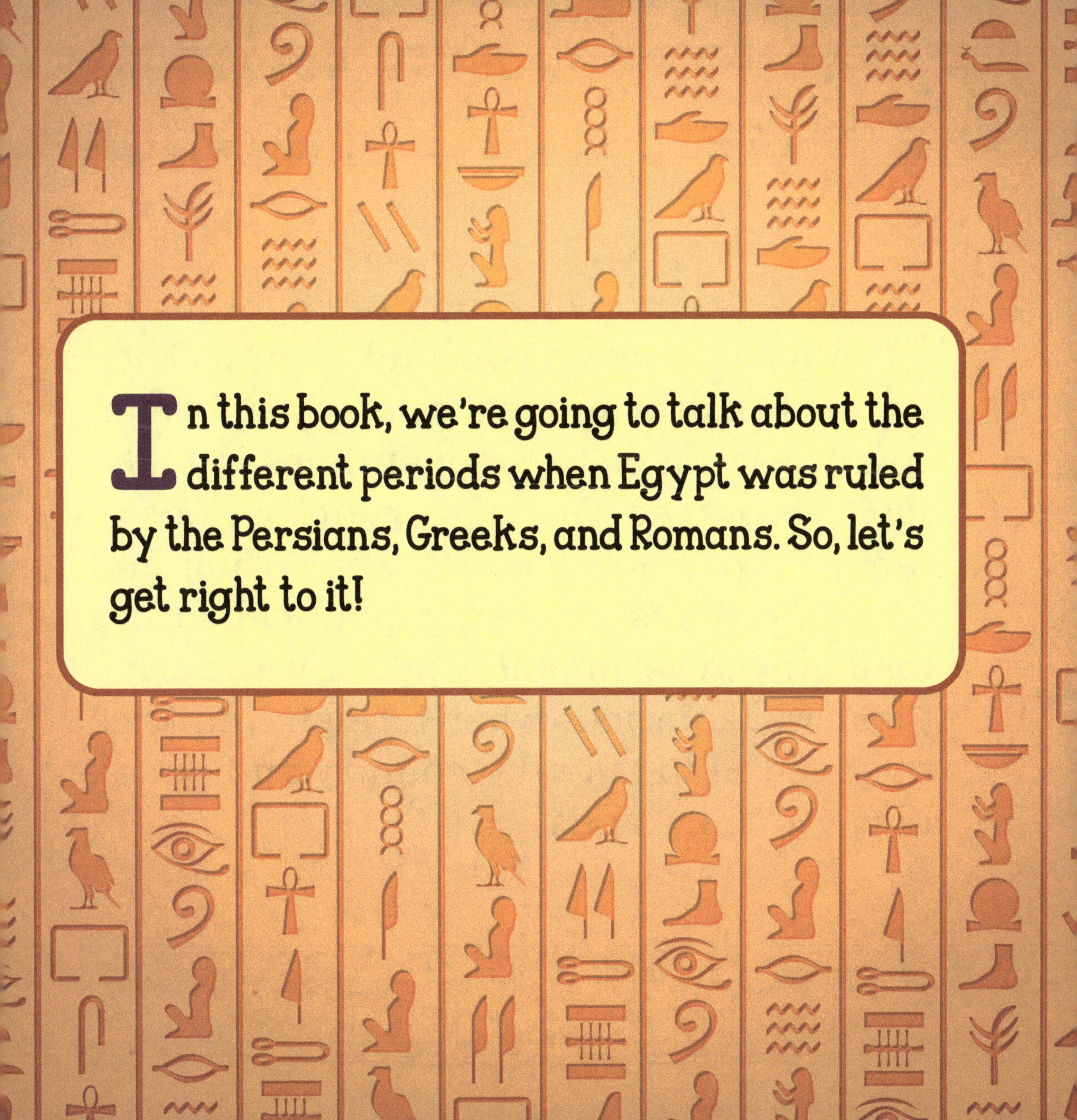

In this book, we're going to talk about the different periods when Egypt was ruled by the Persians, Greeks, and Romans. So, let's get right to it!

The ancient civilization of Egypt lasted almost three thousand years. They were a wealthy empire and other foreign countries wanted to conquer them and take their resources. During certain periods of time, Egypt's government was strong and at other times opposing political forces made the government weak. It was during these weak periods when foreign countries swooped in to take the country and annex Egypt to their lands.

Pyramid of Giza

THE PERSIANS INVADED EGYPT

- Persia conquered Egypt at three different times.
- 525 to 404 Bc: Egypt was conquered by the royal dynasty, the Achaemenids
- 343 to 332 Bc: Egypt was independent from 404 Bc to 343 Bc and then the Achaemenids took over again

619 to 629 AD: After a long period of rule by the Greeks, Romans, and Byzantines, the Persians, in the form of the Sassanid Empire, took over and ruled for 10 years before the invasion of the country by the Muslims.

Bashkirs
Magyars
Kimeks
Utigurs (Bulgars)
Khazars
Onogurs (Bulgars)
22
Alans
Abasgia
Lazic
23
24
Albania
Oghuz?
Kangars
Western
Tokharistan (Hephthalites)
25
28
29
26
27
Persian Empire (Sassanid Dynasty)
Ghassanids
Lakhmids
Sindh (Rais)
Ghatafan
Hanifa
Ghifar
Quraysh
Hawazin
Ka'b
Azd
Azd 'Oman
Kindah
Mahra
Bega
Yemen (Hijaz)
Axum
vassals

A PSYCHOLOGICAL BATTLE

The Late Period of Egypt's history began around 664 BC and ended around 332 BC. During this time, the Assyrians left Egypt. The local governments and people regained control over their country. However, this period of Egypt when it was united against foreign takeover wouldn't last a very long time.

Monastery in Sinai

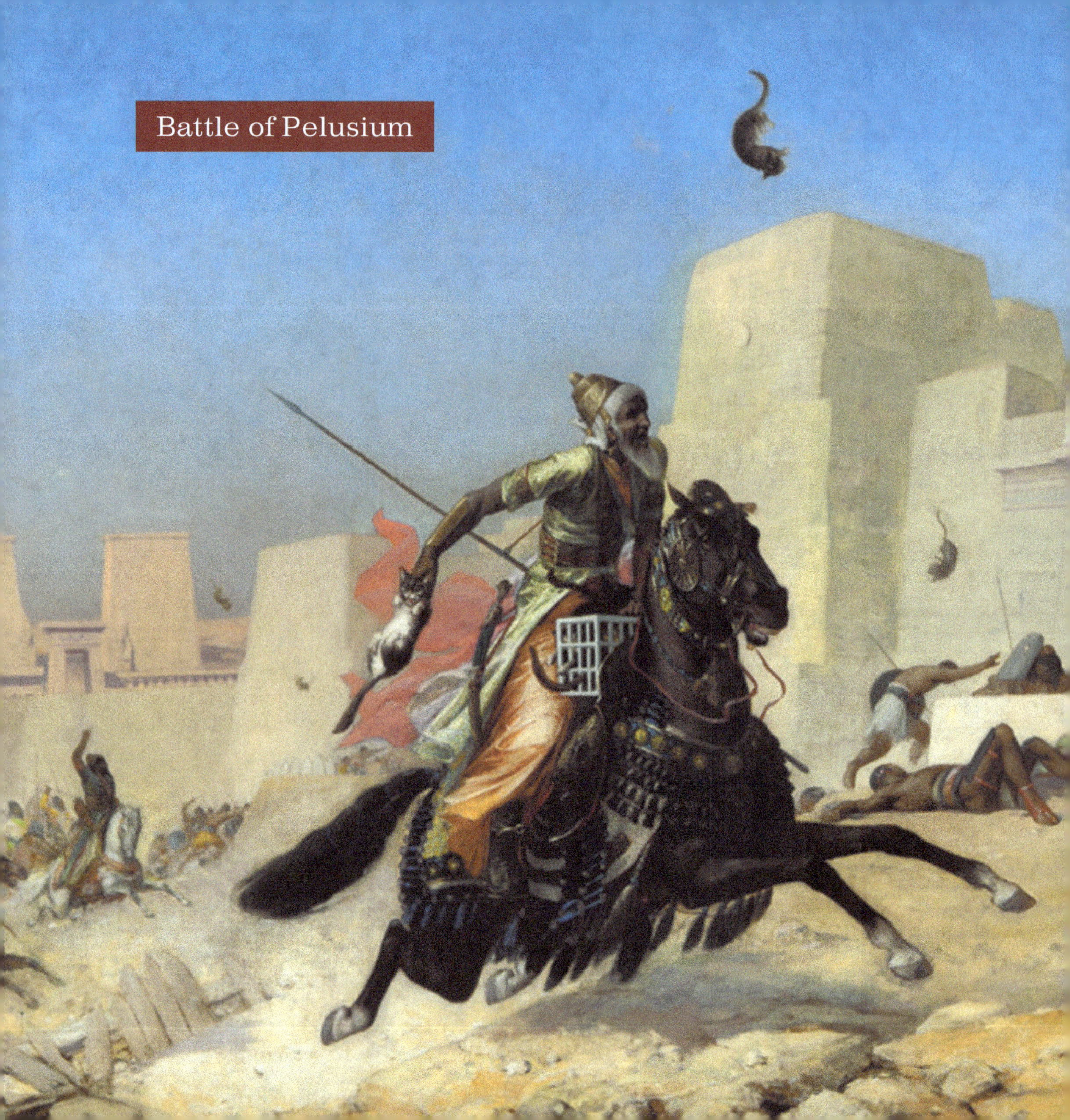

Battle of Pelusium

In the year 525 BC, King Cambyses II led his armies into Egypt and defeated the Egyptian soldiers at a battle fought at Pelusium. This battle is important from a historical perspective. The Persians used a psychological strategy to win the battle. They knew that the Egyptians revered cats.

Their goddess Bastet was pictured with the head of a cat. Bastet, who was the goddess of the home and childbirth, protected their dwellings from evil spirits, just as real-life cats kept the vermin away. King Cambyses came up with a plan.

Bastet

Persian Soldiers

He told his soldiers to paint images of Bastet on their shields. During the battle, the Persian soldiers were preceded by a large group of cats. The Egyptians weren't willing to harm the cats so they surrendered to the Persian troops.

UNDER PERSIAN RULE

When Persia conquered Egypt, its empire, called the Achaemenid Empire, was already the largest in the world. Egypt became a Persian province, which was called a satrapy. The leaders of this satrapy were the 27th dynasty. Persia kept its reign in Egypt for one hundred years.

UVARAZMIS
DAHA
ARMINA
THOSPIA
VARKANA
SUGUDA
GAZAKA
TARSOS
ARBELA
MADA
SALAMIS
EBIR-NARI
ATHURA
YADNANA
GABAI
ARTAKANA
SOUSA
PASARGADAI
ANSAN
PERSEPOLIS
KARMANA
PARSA
POURA
HARMOZEIA
UDRAYA
MAKA
Achaemenid Empire

The Army of Cambyses

The third king of the Achaemenid Empire in Egypt was Darius I. He was later known as Darius the Great. He was twenty-eight years old when he first took the throne.

Darius the Great

He ruled Egypt from 522 BC through 486 Bc. This was during the time when Persia was experiencing its golden age.

He led campaigns to conquer lands in Europe as well as Greece and the Indus valley. He was famous for more than just his military skill. King Darius was a progressive leader who improved the Egyptian legal system and its economic system as well. He also promoted the construction of many building projects throughout the Persian Empire including Egypt.

Xerxes

King Darius had temples built to the Egyptian gods and goddesses. He dressed and presented himself to the people of Egypt as their pharaoh so they would feel comfortable with him. Egypt was prosperous during this era. The later Achaemenid leaders, such as Xerxes, treated the Egyptians with disdain and cruelty.

THE GREEKS INVADED EGYPT

The period of Persian rule ended when famous conqueror Alexander the Great from Greece arrived in 332 BC. Alexander's military campaigns had conquered much of the territory from the Middle East to India.

Alexander the Great

He was victorious against the Persians and brought the spoils of Egypt into his ever-growing empire. The Egyptians saw him as a savior from Persian rule and they offered little resistance to his takeover of Egypt.

Alexander proclaimed himself Pharaoh and founded the capital of Alexandria, which became a global center of culture and learning. He had a great deal of respect for the religion of the Egyptians. He went to the ancient Egyptian city of Memphis and also went to see the oracle of the god Amun located at the Oasis of Siwa.

Alexander the Great Founding Alexandria

Statue of Amun-Re

By now, a great deal of the Egyptian religion had spilled over to other countries and cultures. When the oracle, who was a prophet, saw Alexander, he proclaimed that he was the son of the powerful Egyptian creator god Amun-Re.

After Alexander passed away, one of his top generals Ptolemy I Soter became the ruler of Egypt and this was the start of the Ptolemaic Dynasty in 305 BC. This dynasty was the final dynasty in the history of Ancient Egypt. Although Egypt's rulers were now Greek, they absorbed the Egyptian religion and blended the cultures of Greece and Egypt together.

Ptolemy I Soter

Gerdek Rock Tomb, Hellenistic period

They ruled Egypt for almost 300 years until 30 BC. This period was called the Hellenistic period. Egypt under Ptolemaic rule was a dominant power in the region. The armies of Egypt traveled further east and north than during any other time period of their history.

The city of Alexandria became the center for intellectuals. There was a spirit of exchange between cultures that

promoted advances in science, art, and mathematics. The library had thousands of scrolls from all areas of scholarship.

Egyptian Art

Egyptian art also thrived during this period. Many of the remaining monumental temples still standing in Egypt are from this era. The city was also a major port of trade between the three continents of Asia, Europe, and Africa. The peak of this period was around 240 Bc. The Egyptian empire had expanded and gained power over Libya and Palestine as well as Cyprus and a great portion of the eastern Mediterranean.

The Ptolemaic Dynasty began to crumble when Ptolemy III died in 221 BC. There was corruption in the government and the people were beginning to rebel across the country. During the same period of time, the Roman Empire was starting to get stronger.

Ptolemy III

Statue of Cleopatra VII

THE ROMANS INVADED EGYPT

Perhaps the most famous Pharaoh of the Ptolemaic Dynasty was Cleopatra VII. She had Greek ancestors, was highly intelligent, and spoke nine different languages. She was also a diplomat. She developed an alliance, both romantic and political, with the Roman leader Julius Caesar. They both saw the benefit of uniting their powerful countries.

However, in 44 BC, Caesar was assassinated leaving Cleopatra and Egypt in danger of retaining their independence. Once again, Cleopatra gained an ally when she formed a romantic and political alliance with the Roman commander Mark Antony. They joined forces to fight another Roman leader named Octavian. Octavian was victorious against the Egyptian armies at the Battle of Actium. Octavian eventually renamed himself Augustus and became emperor of Rome.

Julius Caesar

Cleopatra and Antony

Antony and Cleopatra were desperate in their defeat. When Antony heard that Cleopatra had killed herself, he attempted to commit suicide with his own sword, but was brought back to her where he died in her arms. She then committed suicide by allowing herself to be bitten by a venomous snake rather than face what would happen to her if she were captured.

The death of Cleopatra in 30 BC, officially marked the end of the Ptolemaic Dynasty. She was the last pharaoh of Egypt. Cleopatra had a son with Caesar and she tried to hide him, but Octavian, now named Augustus, found him and had him killed. Cleopatra had twins, a girl and a boy with Mark Antony. They also had another son four years after they had the twins. When Cleopatra and Mark Antony died, their children were taken to live with Antony's wife in Rome.

Death of Cleopatra

Surprisingly, the Romans didn't change much about Egyptian daily life. Egypt was important to them because the farms of Egypt provided grain. The country was an

important trade center and was a source of great wealth for the Roman Empire. The Romans ruled Egypt for over 600 years.

PERSIAN RULE ONCE AGAIN

During the Greek period, the rulers of the powerful Ptolemaic kingdom were able to keep the Persians out of Egypt. This was true during the Roman period of rule as well. In the 4th century, Rome was split and Egypt became a part of the Byzantine Empire. Then, the East Romans, called the Byzantines, took over as rulers of Egypt for a period of time.

Byzantines

Relief of Sasanian King Khosrow II

In the 7th century, Egypt's borders were constantly being attacked from the east. It was during the last part of the Byzantine rule that the government was weakened again and the King of Persia, the Sasanian King Khosrow II sent Persian soldiers under the command of the famous military leader Shahrbaraz to take control of Egypt once more in addition to other areas of the Near East. The Persians once again ruled Egypt for a decade from 619 to 629 AD.

MUSLIM CONQUEST OF EGYPT

In 641 AD, the Muslims invaded and took over Egypt. Egypt remained under Arab control through the period of the Middle Ages.

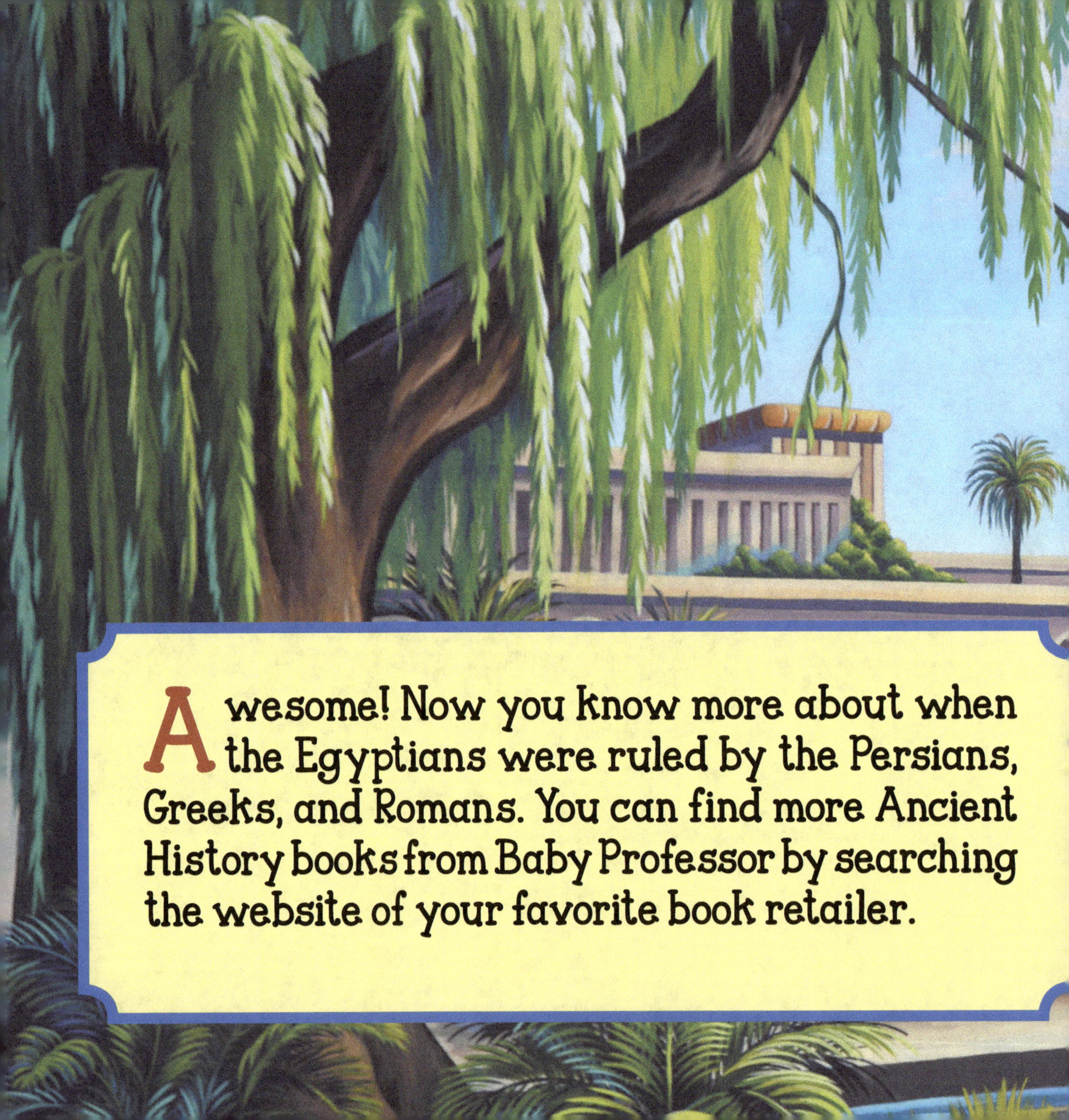

Awesome! Now you know more about when the Egyptians were ruled by the Persians, Greeks, and Romans. You can find more Ancient History books from Baby Professor by searching the website of your favorite book retailer.

Visit
BABY PROFESSOR
EDUCATION KIDS
www.BabyProfessorBooks.com
to download Free Baby Professor eBooks
and view our catalog of new and exciting
Children's Books

www.ingramcontent.com/pod-product-compliance
Lightning Source LLC
LaVergne TN
LVHW060828170826
845678LV00010B/1924
* 9 7 9 8 8 6 9 4 3 1 2 3 3 *